A CENTURY
OF STORIES
NEW HANOVER COUNTY PUBLIC LIBRARY
1906-2006

ATLANTIC OCEAN

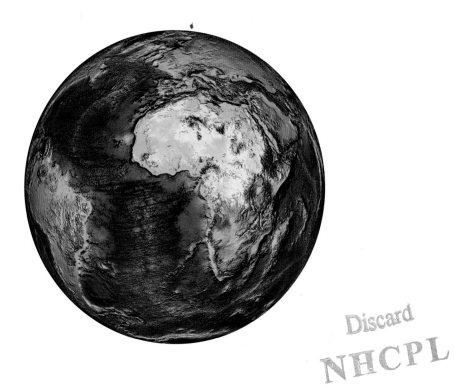

Jen Green

WORLD ALMANAC® LIBRARY

Please visit our web site at: www.worldalmanaclibrary.com
For a free color catalog describing World Almanac® Library's list of
high-quality books and multimedia programs, call 1-800-848-2928 (USA)
or 1-800-387-3178 (Canada). World Almanac® Library's fax: (414) 332-3567.

Library of Congress Cataloging-in-Publication Data

Green, Jen.
    Atlantic Ocean / Jen Green.
        p. cm. — (Oceans and seas)
    Includes bibliographical references and index.
    ISBN 0-8368-6271-6 (lib. bdg.)
    ISBN 0-8368-6279-1 (softcover)
    1. Atlantic Ocean—Juvenile literature.   1. Title.
    GC481.G74   2006
    551.46'13—dc22   20050542928

First published in 2006 by
World Almanac® Library
A Member of the WRC Media Family of Companies
330 West Olive Street, Suite 100
Milwaukee, WI 53212 USA

Produced by Discovery Books
Editor: Sabrina Crewe
Designer and page production: Sabine Beaupré
Photo researcher: Sabrina Crewe
Maps and diagrams: Stefan Chabluk
Geographical consultant: Keith Lye
World Almanac® Library editorial direction: Valerie Weber
World Almanac® Library editor: Gini Holland
World Almanac® Library art direction: Tammy West
World Almanac® Library graphic design: Charlie Dahl
World Almanac® Library production: Jessica Morris and Robert Kraus

Picture credits: Corbis: pp. 28, 39, 41; FLPA: pp. 11, 15, 21, 26, 29, 38, 42; Getty Images:
pp. 6, 10, 12, 18, 24–25, 30, 33, 37; NOAA: cover, pp. 8, 13, 19 (both), 20, 23,
25 (bottom), 27, 31, 32, 35, 36, 40; NOAA/NGDC: title page.

Printed in the United States of America

1 2 3 4 5 6 7 8 9 10 09 08 07 06

CONTENTS

Front cover: *This rocky stretch of coastline along the Atlantic Ocean is in Acadia National Park, Maine.*
Title page: *This computer-generated image of Earth was based on land and ocean measurements made by the U.S. National Geophysical Data Center. This view shows most of the Atlantic Ocean, with the east coast of North America just visible top left.*

Words that appear in the glossary are printed in **boldface** the first time they occur in text.

The Atlantic Ocean is the world's second largest ocean after the Pacific. It covers almost 30 million square miles (almost 77 million square kilometers), making it more than six times the size of the United States. The ocean is probably named after Atlas, a giant from Greek mythology who supported the world on his shoulders.

Boundaries of the Atlantic

The Atlantic is shaped like a vast letter "S" that narrows in the middle, near the **equator**. The two widest parts are the North Atlantic and South Atlantic. The great landmasses of the Americas form the ocean's western boundary, while Europe and Africa border it to the east. The Arctic Ocean lies to the north and the Southern Ocean to the south. The Atlantic includes many seas and other bodies of water. The Caribbean Sea and **Gulf** of Mexico are in the ocean's western part, while the Mediterranean and Black Seas are in the eastern part. The North Sea, Baltic Sea, Norwegian Sea, and Labrador Sea are all in the northern Atlantic, and most of the Scotia Sea is within the ocean's southern boundary. An area of calm, warm water named the Sargasso Sea lies near the center of the Atlantic Ocean.

At **Cape** Horn, on the southern tip of South America, Atlantic waters mingle with those of the Pacific. The Atlantic meets the Indian Ocean at the Cape of Good Hope on the southern tip of Africa.

A Busy Ocean

The Atlantic is a vast expanse of water spanning the northern and southern hemispheres. The ocean has been important for trade since the 1600s, and it is still the world's busiest ocean. Many large

Living Resources

"We've always treated the ocean like a frontier, as if its resources were infinite and free to plunder. And several centuries ago, that may effectively have been true. However, humankind is now mining the oceans's living resources, making them nonrenewable. . . . We must learn how to use them sustainably— by understanding and respecting their biology."

Elliott Norse, president of the Marine Conservation Biology Insititute, quoted in an article about overfishing, "Empty Nets" by Janet Raloff, Science News, *June 2005*

Atlantic Ocean Key Facts

Surface area:
29,638,000 square
miles (76,762,000
sq km)

Coastline: 69,514 miles
(111,866 kilometers)

Average depth: 12,880
feet (3,926 meters)

Deepest known point:
Milwaukee Deep in
the Puerto Rico
Trench, 28,232 feet
(8,605 m)

industrial nations have
grown up on its shores.
The Atlantic is rich in
resources, including fish
and **minerals**. In recent
years, however, **overfishing**
has greatly reduced stocks
of Atlantic fish, while
coastal development and
industry have caused several
kinds of pollution. The
floor of the Atlantic has
now been charted, but
many mysteries still lie
in the ocean's depths.

*This map shows the Atlantic Ocean,
its major islands and underwater
features, and the landmasses that
border it.*

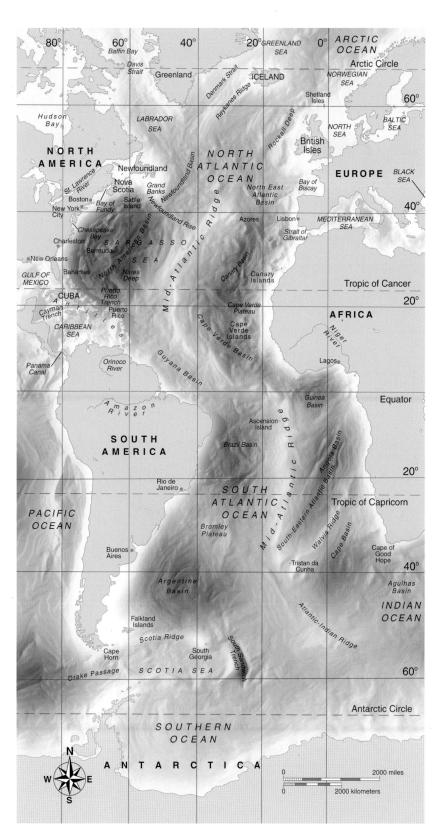

CHAPTER ONE

PHYSICAL FEATURES

The Atlantic Ocean is nearly 2.5 miles (4 km) deep on average. The ocean bed, however, is far from smooth and flat. On the contrary, it has towering mountains and plunging chasms higher and deeper than any on land. These features were mostly formed by movements of giant slabs of rock, known as tectonic plates, which make up Earth's outer layers. These movements and other factors ensure that the Atlantic Ocean is still changing today.

Formation

Scientists believe the Atlantic Ocean began to take shape around 190 million years ago. Movements of Earth's tectonic plates caused a **rift** to open up between North America and landmasses to the east, including Asia, Africa, and Europe. As this great valley widened, it filled with water to become the North Atlantic. Later, another rift opened to separate South America and Africa, forming the South Atlantic.

The Mid-Atlantic Ridge

The Atlantic's most dramatic feature is an enormous chain of mountains, running right down the center, called the Mid-Atlantic **Ridge**. About 930 miles (1,496 km) wide, it is part of a world-wide undersea ridge system and is the world's longest mountain chain. The ridge rears 0.6–2 miles (1–3 km) above

Iceland in the North Atlantic is part of the Mid-Atlantic Ridge. This aerial view shows craters formed there by the kind of volcanic eruptions that also take place underwater.

Plates and Oceans

Earth's outer layers are made up of a number of vast, rigid sections called tectonic plates—seven major ones and up to twelve smaller ones. Fitting together like pieces of a jigsaw puzzle, the plates underlie oceans and dry land. The plates drift across Earth's surface, floating on a lower, molten layer of the **mantle** like chunks of bread on a thick, bubbling soup. As they drift, tectonic plates can push together, grind past one another, or pull apart.

Volcanic eruptions and earthquakes are common along plate boundaries because the crust is thinnest there. Where two plates pull apart, as is happening in the center of the Atlantic, **magma** rises to fill the space, creating a mountain chain underwater or on land. Elsewhere, plates collide. Where this happens, one plate may dive below the other to form a deep trench, such as the Puerto Rico Trench bordering the Caribbean.

About 250 million years ago, Earth's landmasses were united in a single "super-continent" named Pangaea, which was surrounded by a vast ocean now known as Panthalassa. About 200 million years ago, because of **continental drift** caused by plate movement, a great bay—the Tethys Sea—opened up in the center of Pangaea and split it in half. The northern landmass—named Laurasia—included North America, Greenland, Europe, and Asia, while the southern half—Gondwanaland—included South America, Africa, India, Australia, and Antarctica. As plate movement continued over millions of years, the continents and oceans took their present positions (shown below with the major tectonic plates), and they continue to shift today.

the surrounding ocean bed. Even at that height, most summits along the ridge still lie well below the surface, but in places, they jut out of the water to form islands.

The Mid-Atlantic Ridge marks the border between some of Earth's tectonic plates that are very slowly drifting in opposite directions. In the center of

Hydrothermal Vents

In 1977, scientists exploring the ocean depths in **submersibles** made an amazing discovery. In a rift valley on a deep-ocean ridge in the Pacific, they came upon extraordinary rock chimneys belching clouds of scalding water, black with the minerals sulfur and iron. These hydrothermal vents, also called "black smokers," are now thought to occur in volcanically active regions in many parts of the oceans, and several have been found in the Atlantic Ocean. At these sites, ocean water entering cracks in the crust is heated and mixed with newly erupted minerals to gush out again in dark clouds of hot water. The minerals settle and build up around the vents to form chimneys. They also seep out into the ocean, adding to the water's salt levels. "White smokers" have also been found. These vents spew slightly cooler water containing white minerals. The largest group of vents discovered so far lies on the Mid-Atlantic Ridge. The size of a football field, the hydrothermal site is named the Transatlantic Geotraverse.

A hydrothermal vent spews scalding black smoke deep in the Atlantic Ocean.

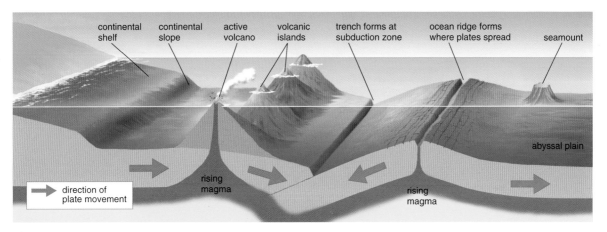

continental shelf | continental slope | active volcano | volcanic islands | trench forms at subduction zone | ocean ridge forms where plates spread | seamount | abyssal plain | direction of plate movement | rising magma | rising magma

This diagram shows some of the features that form on Earth's ocean floors.

the ridge is a rift valley where molten rock oozes up from below to fill the gap between the plates. In some areas along this long, deep valley, scientists have discovered **hydrothermal vents** that gush clouds of hot, mineral-rich water.

Spreading Outward

In the 1960s, a drilling ship named *Glomar Challenger* took rock samples from the floor of the Atlantic Ocean. Geologists learned that the rocks in the center, at the Mid-Atlantic Ridge, were the youngest in the ocean, with progressively older rocks to either side. They concluded that the ocean floor was spreading from the center, along plate boundaries, as newly erupted rock pushed older rocks aside toward the edges of the ocean. Because of this movement, it appears, the Atlantic Ocean is growing wider every year, by 0.5 to 0.8 inches (1 to 2 centimeters).

Ups and Downs

As well as the Mid-Atlantic Ridge, the bed of the Atlantic also has smaller ridges and other areas of high ground called rises. These high areas divide the ocean floor into a series of basins, or abyssal plains. Deep trenches, known as **subduction zones**, occur along plate borders where two plates collide and one is forced below the other. The Milwaukee Deep in the Puerto Rico Trench, north of the island of Puerto Rico, is the deepest known point in the Atlantic Ocean.

Near the edges of the ocean, abyssal plains slope upward to the shallow waters that edge the world's continents. These rocky ledges are known as continental shelves. In the Atlantic, they are at their widest—up to 300 miles (480 km) wide—off the coasts of North America, Europe, and southern South America. The continental shelves edging West Africa and northern South America are narrower, only about 100 miles (160 km) wide.

Islands

The Atlantic has relatively few islands compared to the Pacific. Atlantic islands range in size from tiny specks in the

ocean to large landmasses, such as Newfoundland. As in other oceans, there are two main types of islands in the Atlantic: continental and oceanic.

Continental islands rise from the shallow waters of continental shelves. They include Newfoundland and the British Isles. These and most other continental islands were once part of the nearby mainland. They formed because of changes in sea level, which in turn are linked to long-term climate change. During long, cold periods called ice ages, sea levels are generally lower than usual because so much water is locked up

A rocky cliff rises out of the Atlantic in the Orkney Islands off the coast of Scotland. The British Isles, including the Orkney Islands, are continental islands that were once part of the European landmass.

as ice. Ice ages are interspersed with warmer periods when the ice melts, swelling the oceans and causing sea levels to rise. Scientists believe the last ice age ended between ten and twenty thousand years ago. As the climate started to warm, rising seas began to flood the low-lying area between Britain and the rest of Europe. Eventually, Great Britain and Ireland became islands.

Oceanic Islands

Oceanic islands are often far from any mainland. They are mostly formed by volcanic activity as undersea volcanoes ooze **lava** that builds up to form rocky peaks called seamounts. Eventually, so much lava builds up that the peaks break through the water's surface to become islands. In the Atlantic Ocean, the Azores, Tristan da Cunha, and the large island of Iceland are all tips of volcanic peaks located on the Mid-Atlantic Ridge, along the border between tectonic plates.

Elsewhere, an arc of volcanic islands sometimes rises above the waves along a subduction zone. At these sites, one tectonic plate is descending beneath another. As the plate descends, its forward edge melts, creating magma that rises to form a chain of volcanic islands. Islands formed in this way include the Lesser Antilles in the western Atlantic.

The island of Surtsey formed in 1963–1965 after the eruption of an underwater volcano. About 1.25 square miles (3.2 sq km) in size, Surtsey is in the North Atlantic.

Smooth beaches stretch along the coast of Benin in Africa.

The Southern Ocean

The most southern waters of the Atlantic Ocean meet those of the Southern Ocean. Until 2000, part of the Southern Ocean was included within the boundaries of the Atlantic Ocean, but the Southern Ocean was then officially declared separate. The Southern Ocean stretches across 7,848,255 square miles (20,327,000 sq km) of Earth's most southern region, surrounding the icy continent of Antarctica. Much of the ocean is covered by ice in winter. With its strong winds and freezing temperatures, the Southern Ocean is inhospitable to human settlement, but some animals also found in the Atlantic Ocean, including species of penguins and seals, live there.

Coasts

Along the eastern rim of the Atlantic, the combined coasts of Europe and Africa stretch for 32,000 miles (51,500 km). In the west, the coastlines of the Americas add up to 55,000 miles (88,500 km). Atlantic coasts hold a huge variety of coastal features. The coasts of South America and Africa are fairly smooth and regular, with long, sweeping beaches. North America and much of Europe have highly irregular coastlines indented with deep bays and inlets. These areas make fine natural harbors. The coasts of Newfoundland, Nova Scotia, and Maine are generally rugged, with many small islands. South of New York, **barrier islands** and sand **spits** are common. Both of these land features are formed from rock or sand brought by **currents** and waves.

Shaping Coastlines

The huge variety of natural features found on coasts are shaped by two main processes: erosion and deposition. Erosion is the wearing away of the land by water, wind, and other natural forces. Deposition is the laying down of rocky materials, or deposits, often in the form of fine particles, such as sand or mud.

Waves are the main force of erosion on coastlines. As they beat against the shore, they hurl sand and **shingle** against rocks to wear them away. Bands of hard rock at the water's edge are left to form jutting headlands, while soft rocks are eaten away to form deep, curving bays. In some areas, waves eat into coasts by 3 feet (1 m) or more each year, gradually shifting the shore inland.

Out to sea, the pounding waves smash rocky fragments into sand and shingle. Coastal currents may carry these materials for miles along the shore and then deposit them to form beaches and spits. The coasts of Brazil and West Africa have some of the world's longest beaches, which were formed by this type of deposition. Elsewhere, at river mouths, **sediment** carried down by rivers is dropped to form flat, swampy **deltas**. The Amazon Delta in South America was formed in this way and is one of the largest in the world.

Atlantic coasts and islands have also been shaped by changing ocean levels over the last twenty thousand years. Water levels have been steadily rising, and Atlantic water has flooded land around **estuaries**, creating inlets with many forks. These estuaries include Chesapeake Bay, the largest in the United States.

An artificial barrier (right) along the shoreline of Chesapeake Bay helps to lessen erosion by waves.

CHAPTER TWO

CLIMATE AND CURRENTS

Seawater is not the same throughout the world's oceans. Some waters are saltier than others. The waters of the open Atlantic Ocean are relatively low in salt compared to some of its more enclosed areas, such as the Mediterranean Sea. The lower salt level is due to the fresh waters of mighty rivers, such as the Amazon and Niger, which feed the Atlantic's coastal waters in many areas. The Atlantic, however, is slightly saltier than both the Pacific Ocean and the Indian Ocean.

Why Is the Ocean Salty?

Ocean water is salty because it contains dissolved minerals, or salts, washed from the land by rivers or released underwater from hydrothermal vents and volcanic eruptions. The salt level in ocean water is higher than in rivers because, when surface water evaporates, the dissolved salts remain in the oceans and become more concentrated. Experts calculate that the salt in all the seas and oceans would be enough to bury Earth's landmasses to a depth of 500 feet (152 m)! So why do oceans and seas not get increasingly salty as new minerals are added each year? Some salt is removed from the water when it is absorbed by marine life or reacts with underwater rock and eventually forms new sediment layers on the ocean floor. These processes help keep salt levels constant in the oceans.

Water Temperatures

Temperatures vary in different parts of the oceans, mainly depending on **latitude**, or distance from the equator. As in other oceans, Atlantic surface waters are warmest—about 80° Fahrenheit (27° Celsius)—in a broad belt around the equator because the Sun's heat is strongest here. The water gets progressively cooler at higher latitudes, dropping to about freezing in **subpolar** regions. Temperatures also vary with depth, with surface waters being warmest. Even in the **Tropics**, the deep waters are very cold.

Winds

The world's winds are bent by Earth's eastward rotation, curving clockwise north of the equator and counterclockwise south of the equator. This is called

the Coriolis Effect. Atlantic waters are affected by three main belts of wind that blow worldwide in **tropical**, polar, and **temperate** regions. In the Tropics, powerful winds, called trade winds, blow from the northeast and southeast toward the equator. At the equator itself is a belt of very weak winds called the doldrums, where sailing ships often became stranded without strong winds to help them travel.

Currents

The waters of the Atlantic are always on the move. Seawater continually circulates in powerful currents that flow like mighty rivers. Surface currents flowing across the oceans are driven by winds blowing at the surface. In the North and South Atlantic, **prevailing winds** cause the water to flow around in two giant circles called **gyres**.

Strong ocean winds can move sailboats at a fast pace. Winds are named for the direction from which they are blowing. In the temperate regions north and south of the Tropics, the prevailing winds are westerlies; in polar regions, icy, easterly winds blow.

Major currents of the North Atlantic include the cold Canary Current flowing southward, and the North Equatorial Current moving westward. The most important current is the powerful, warm Gulf Stream, which flows northward from the Caribbean. It moves north along the eastern shore of North America, warming coastal regions. Off Cape Hatteras in North Carolina, the Gulf Stream meets the cold waters of the Labrador Current, which have flowed south from the Arctic Ocean. This current cools the eastern coast of Canada

The Water Cycle

Moisture continually circulates between the oceans, air, and land. This never-ending process, called the water cycle, is illustrated below. The Sun beating down on the ocean surface causes moisture to rise into the air in the form of a gas, water vapor. This process of turning liquid into gas is called **evaporation**. As the warm, moist air rises, it cools. Cold air can hold less moisture than warm air, and so the moisture in it **condenses** to form clouds, which may drift over the land before shedding rain. When rain falls on land, any moisture not absorbed by plants or soil drains away into streams and rivers. The water then runs into the ocean to begin the cycle again.

there are lighter. The loop includes the warm Brazil Current flowing south along the coast of South America and the cold Benguela Current flowing north along southwest Africa. In the far south, the icy Antarctic Circumpolar Current flows westward along the border of the Atlantic and Southern Oceans.

Deepwater Currents

In the ocean depths, deepwater currents often flow in the opposite direction to surface waters. These currents are driven by differences in density of various water masses. Cold water that is also salty is denser than warm or less salty water, so these cold water masses sink. This sinking starts a flow of bottom water. In the far north and south of the Atlantic, cold water sinks and then flows

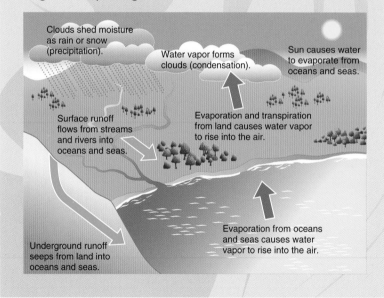

Clouds shed moisture as rain or snow (precipitation).

Water vapor forms clouds (condensation).

Sun causes water to evaporate from oceans and seas.

Surface runoff flows from streams and rivers into oceans and seas.

Evaporation and transpiration from land causes water vapor to rise into the air.

Evaporation from oceans and seas causes water vapor to rise into the air.

Underground runoff seeps from land into oceans and seas.

and sometimes brings icebergs that drift a long way south. The Gulf Stream veers eastward across the Atlantic Ocean before branching into other currents that warm the waters and climate of western Europe.

The huge, counterclockwise gyre in the South Atlantic is less powerful than the North Atlantic gyre because winds

along the bottom toward the equator. There, it warms, rises, and then starts back toward the poles again. When surface water sinks to the bottom of the ocean, it increases oxygen levels in the depths, which benefits deepwater creatures. **Upwellings**, where cold, mineral-rich water is rising, support

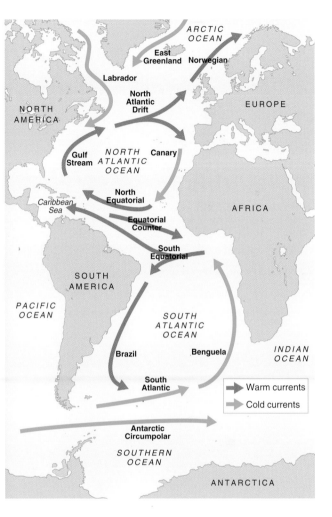

This map shows the major surface currents of the Atlantic Ocean.

an abundance of life near the surface. Upwellings off the coast of West Africa and off the Namibian coast in southwest Africa have created rich fishing grounds.

Atlantic Tides

The Atlantic's tidal range, or variation in water level at the coasts, is often greatest in deep inlets and bays. In the Bay of Fundy in Nova Scotia, the water changes by an average of 47.5 feet (14.5 m)

What Causes Tides?

Tides are regular rises and falls in sea level caused mainly by the tug of the Moon's gravity. As the Moon orbits Earth, its gravity pulls ocean water into a mound below it. A similar bulge appears on the ocean on the opposite side of Earth because the planet itself is also being pulled, by the same force, away from the water on the far side. As Earth spins eastward, so the mounds move westward across Earth's surface, bringing tides to coasts in succession. Because Earth spins around once every twenty-four hours, the two bulges both move across Earth once in that period, creating two tides a day in each place. The tides are not always equal in volume, however. In some parts of more enclosed seas, such as the Gulf of Mexico, there is just one tide a day.

The Sun's gravity exerts a similar, but weaker, pull on the oceans. This is because, while many times larger than the Moon, it is also much farther away. Every two weeks, at the full moon and again during the new moon, the Sun and Moon line up so that their pulls combine. This force brings extra-high tides called spring tides. They alternate with weaker tides also occurring every two weeks, called neap tides, when the two pulls tend to minimize each other.

between high tide and low tide—one of the world's greatest tidal ranges. Tidal waters also swirl far upriver to affect inland areas. Tidewaters moving up the St. Lawrence River in Canada, for example, reach as far as 930 miles (1,496 km) inland.

Waves

Waves are moving ridges of water that vary in size from small ripples to towering walls of water. They are caused by winds blowing across the ocean surface. In some parts of the Atlantic—such as the Bay of Biscay off Spain, Cape Horn at the tip of

In September 2004, huge waves created by Hurricane Jeanne (shown here) battered the coast of Florida, causing flooding, tearing off roofs, and felling trees. It was the fourth hurricane to hit the state in a period of six weeks.

South America, and the coast of Namibia in southwestern Africa—strong winds and currents regularly cause rough seas.

Climate

The vast north-to-south extent of the Atlantic means that it spans a huge range of climates, from tropical to subpolar. Like other oceans, it has a generally moderating influence on the climates of coastal regions, making summers cooler and winters milder than they are farther inland. Ocean currents, however, vary this general pattern. Warm currents, such as the Gulf Stream, bring warmer conditions throughout the year; while cold currents, such as the Benguela Current, chill land as they flow past it. Where warm and cold ocean currents meet, as they do at the Grand Banks off Newfoundland, fogs are common.

Atlantic Hurricanes

The warm waters of the Tropics are breeding grounds for hurricanes from July to October. The huge, spinning storms begin far out in the ocean, at centers of **low pressure** where warm, moist air is rising upward. As the rising air cools, its moisture condenses, bringing lashing rain and releasing heat that fuels the developing storm. Winds begin to spiral faster and faster around the center of low pressure, which becomes the calm "eye" in the center of the hurricane. The winds and waves created by hurricanes cause huge damage when they reach coasts. Atlantic hurricanes usually strike the southeastern United States, the Gulf of Mexico, and the islands of the Caribbean. Sometimes, fierce winds around the hurricane's eye cause seawater to pile up and form a mound of water called a storm surge, which can hit ocean shores in a gigantic wave with an impact similar to a tsunami.

In 2005, the Atlantic hurricane season began with two hurricanes in July followed by the huge Hurricane Katrina in August. Katrina's storm surges ravaged Biloxi and Gulfport in Mississippi and other places along the Gulf of Mexico coast. Winds and flooding took many lives and destroyed buildings in Mississippi, Alabama, and Louisiana. Rising water caused by the hurricane then broke through flood barriers in New Orleans and filled the city, bringing widespread death and devastation. The hurricane seriously impacted the U.S. economy, not just in New Orleans and along the Gulf, but across the nation as shipping and oil production were interrupted.

A large vessel was pushed ashore by Hurricane Katrina in Plaquemines Parish, Louisiana. The roofs of flooded houses are visible bottom left.

CHAPTER THREE

MARINE LIFE

The vast spaces of the Atlantic Ocean offer a wide range of **habitats** for wildlife. Each part of the ocean is home to a particular community of living things. For example, over two thousand species of plants and animals live in the Gulf of Maine alone. As in other oceans, the Atlantic has two main types of habitat— the shallow coastal waters and the open ocean. The open ocean divides into several more zones, each occurring at a different depth. Coastal habitats are rich in wildlife, but the open ocean is so vast that it contains a high proportion of Atlantic life.

Coastal Habitats

Coastal habitats of the Atlantic Ocean include river estuaries, **lagoons**, and **marshes**, which contain a mixture of fresh and salty water. In the Tropics, forests of mangrove trees grow at the water's edge. At low tide, their knobbly, stilt-like roots stick out of the mud, which allows the trees to breathe. Along the east coast of the United States, the still waters of lagoons and swamps are nurseries for fish and shellfish. Cockles, tubeworms, and razor shells live in the sediment of mudflats and sandy beaches, while crabs, limpets, and anemones thrive in pools on the Atlantic ocean's rocky shores.

Zones of the Open Ocean

The open waters of the Atlantic may be divided into three main habitats, each with different conditions in terms

*Coral **reefs**, such as this one in coastal North Carolina, form in warm, shallow waters. Made of the shell-like remains of millions of **polyps**, coral reefs shelter colorful fish, crabs, and sponges.*

of light, oxygen, and water temperature. The **euphotic zone**, or upper waters, extends from the surface to 330–660 feet (100–200 m) deep. These warm, sunlit, oxygen-rich waters support seaweeds and floating **plankton**, which feed shrimp, jellyfish, and surface-dwelling fish.

The **bathyal zone**, in the middle depths, stretches from 330–660 feet to 6,600 feet (100–200 m to 2,000 m) down. The upper part of this region is sometimes known as the "twilight zone" because some sunlight filters down.

No light reaches the waters of the **abyssal zone** below 6,600 feet (2,000 m). Creatures there feed on the remains of plants and animals that drift down from above, or they prey upon each other.

Hydrothermal vents in the deep ocean are home to unusual species of blind crabs, clams, and tiny fish. Unlike almost all other living things, these creatures do not depend on sunlight or oxygen for energy. Instead, the food chain at the vents is based on bacteria that thrive in the hot, mineral-rich water gushing out of the volcanic openings.

Plant Life

Plant life of the Atlantic includes sea grasses, such as eel and cord grass, which

The female deep-sea anglerfish has a lure, resembling live prey, protruding above its eyes to attract other predators. The anglerfish's huge mouth and expandable stomach can accommodate quite large creatures that are fooled by this bait into coming within range.

grow in sand or mud by the water's edge. Where the grasses become well established, they create coastal marshes. Like other plants, marine plants need sunlight to survive. Some seaweeds live in the sunlit shallows, where they anchor onto rocks using root-like structures called holdfasts. Other types of seaweed float at the ocean surface using air-filled bladders. In the western Atlantic, huge clumps of brown sargassum weed drift in the warm waters of the Sargasso Sea.

Tiny plant plankton also live at the sunlit surface. These microscopic plants are most plentiful in waters that are rich

Ocean Food Chains

In the Atlantic, as in other oceans, living things depend on one another for food. The relationships between plants and animals in a habitat can be shown in a food chain. Plants form the base of almost all marine food chains. Seaweeds and microscopic floating plants called phytoplankton use light to make their food, through the process of **photosynthesis**. Tiny animals called zooplankton, including young fish and shellfish, feed on plant plankton. In turn, the zooplankton provide food for larger creatures. Powerful hunters, such as swordfish, dolphins, and sharks, form the top of the food chain. When these and other living things die, their remains are eaten by scavenging shrimps, crabs, and microbes. This process helps to recycle the energy their bodies contain.

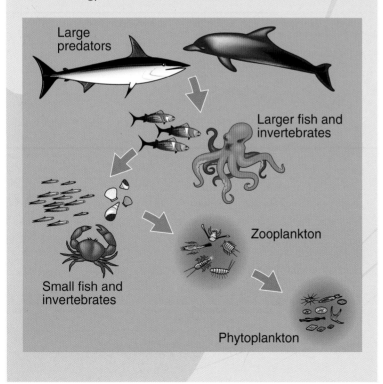

Large predators

Larger fish and invertebrates

Zooplankton

Small fish and invertebrates

Phytoplankton

in nutrients. Plankton thrive in coastal waters—where rivers deposit rich sediment from the land—and also out at sea in upwellings, where cold currents bring minerals up from deep water. Such sites include the coast of Namibia. Plankton also abound in the far North and South Atlantics in spring and summer, when the long daylight hours cause the tiny plants to "bloom," or multiply. This seasonal plenty brings all kinds of creatures, including great whales, to these waters to feed.

Invertebrates

Scientists divide both marine animals and land animals into two main groups: vertebrates, which possess a bony inner skeleton including a backbone, and invertebrates, which have no backbone. Atlantic waters include thousands of invertebrates, including jellyfish, anemones, starfish, sponges, and sea urchins. Invertebrates include **mollusks**—such as mussels, scallops, squid, and octopuses—and **crustaceans** including lobsters, shrimps, and crabs. Many of these animals are filter feeders that filter small creatures from

This wolf fish, a vertebrate, is hiding in rocks on the ocean floor off the coast of Massachusetts. Sea anemones (top and left), which are invertebrates, have attached themselves to the rocks, where they wait for prey.

the water through the mouth or another body part. Octopus and sea anemones are lurking hunters, trapping prey in their tentacles. Creatures such as mussels and anemones spend their lives on the ocean bottom and move about very little. Octopuses, crabs, and lobsters move about more freely. Spiny lobsters travel up to 60 miles (96 km) along the coast of Florida, crawling along the ocean bed in long chains.

Fish and Reptiles

The Atlantic Ocean is home to several thousand kinds of vertebrates, including fish, reptiles, birds, and mammals. There are hundreds of different types of fish, varying in size from tiny anchovies to giant whale sharks. Species such as plaice, skates, and rays have flattened bodies that suit them to life on the ocean bed. Herring and mackerel swim near the surface. They have dark upper bodies and pale bellies, which makes it difficult for enemies to spot them either from above or below.

Sharks, tuna, and swordfish are large, fast fish that prey on smaller species, such

Atlantic Migration

Many Atlantic birds, mammals, fish, and reptiles undertake regular migrations each year. Atlantic salmon and eels are unusual in that they migrate only a few times during their lives. North Atlantic salmon spend their adult lives feeding in the cold waters off Greenland and Scandinavia, but they swim up rivers on both sides of the Atlantic to lay their eggs. Later, the young fish make their way back to the sea. Eels make a similar journey, but in the opposite direction. The adults swim all the way from the rivers and lakes of Europe and North America to the Sargasso Sea, where they lay eggs. When the elvers (young eels) hatch, they spend up to three years drifting northward, carried by the Gulf Stream, before making their way to their feeding grounds upriver.

The black-browed albatross breeds in large groups in the Falkland Islands of the South Atlantic. Each year, the birds return to sit on the same mud nests and lay one large egg each. When their chicks are ready to fly in May, the albatross migrate northward until September.

as anchovies and herring. These small fish swim in large, shimmering schools, which makes it more difficult for predators to single them out. Atlantic salmon and eels are among the animals that swim on long **migrations** as they move from their feeding grounds to breeding sites.

Among marine reptiles, many turtles also make long breeding migrations. Atlantic green turtles swim 990 miles (1,592 km) from Brazilian waters to the beaches of Ascension Island in the mid-Atlantic, where they lay their eggs. This journey represents an amazing feat of **navigation**, and scientists do not fully understand how migrants find their way.

Atlantic Birds

Hundreds of different types of birds live in and around the Atlantic Ocean.

scooping fish from the surface. Terns and gannets plunge into the water to catch fish, while penguins and puffins pursue their prey underwater. Waders sift through the mud at the water's edge.

Mammals of the Ocean

Atlantic waters are also home to dozens of mammal species, including seals, whales, and the manatee, which dwells in coastal waters and estuaries in West Africa as well as the Caribbean and Florida. Manatees are slow-moving plant eaters, while all seals and sea lions are carnivores that chase after darting fish. Whales of Atlantic waters include toothed whales of all sizes, from dolphins, belugas, and orcas to the sperm whale. This huge hunter dives down to 4,000 feet (1,219 m) in search of its prey, the deep-sea squid. Baleen whales, named for the baleen plates in their mouths with which they filter their food, are generally bigger than toothed whales. They include Earth's largest living creature, the blue whale, as well as humpback, bowhead, and fin whales.

Atlantic seabirds, such as albatross, spend almost all of their lives on the wing, wheeling over the open ocean. Even these effortless fliers, however, must come ashore to rear their young. In springtime, Atlantic cliffs, dunes, marshes, and mudflats echo with the cries of millions of nesting birds. Many species, including knots and terns, make long breeding migrations across the Atlantic Ocean.

Sea and shore birds use various techniques to catch their food, which includes fish, shrimps, and worms. Skimmers swoop low over the water,

Humpback whales surface with huge mouthfuls of water and shrimp. They strain the water out through the baleen plates that hang down inside their mouths, trapping the prey inside and then swallowing it.

CHAPTER FOUR

PEOPLE AND SETTLEMENT

Humans have been living on the shores of the Atlantic for tens of thousands of years. In early times, people moved to Atlantic coasts to take advantage of the plentiful foods there, including fish, crabs, and birds. They fished in coastal waters, and early settlements grew up on bays and inlets that made good natural harbors. Somewhat later, when people learned how to build boats, the ocean offered a means of transportation.

In many parts of the Atlantic region, coastal climates are milder and wetter than the island regions. Coasts are important to people living in dry regions, such as southwest Africa, where sea fogs help provide moisture for crops.

Early Human Settlement

Humans inhabited the Atlantic coast of Africa as long as 100,000 years ago. Fossils dating from this period show that people there hunted fish and penguins and gathered shellfish. From Africa,

The people of this village in Senegal, Africa, fish using pirogues, a type of canoe. African coasts were home to the earliest Atlantic peoples.

humans eventually moved north into Europe and Asia. The Atlantic coasts of Europe were generally inhabited by about 40,000 years ago, although people were living along coasts of the eastern Mediterranean long before that. About 10,000 years ago, people living along the Fertile Crescent, including the eastern Mediterranean coastal area, began to farm. Historians think they may have been the world's first farmers. Gradually, agriculture spread to eastern Atlantic coasts.

Coastal Peoples of the Americas

People were living on the shores of the Americas at least 15,000 years ago and perhaps much earlier. Native American groups lived by hunting, fishing coastal waters and rivers, and later by raising crops, such as corn, beans, and squash. Some of these early people skimmed the seas in bark canoes. Many coastal peoples lived in longhouses built of timber cut from nearby woodlands. Others lived in huts covered with bark or grasses. In South America, coastal lands near the mighty Amazon and Orinoco Rivers were some of the first parts of the continent to be farmed.

Island Peoples

In ancient times, some Atlantic islands were reached and settled by coastal peoples. The Bahamas, off the coast of Florida, were colonized by the

Arawak people more than 4,500 years ago. The Guanche people from North Africa settled the Canary Islands.

Settlement of the Canary Islands

The first inhabitants of the Canary Islands in the eastern Atlantic were the Guanches. These fair-skinned people probably reached the islands from North Africa around 100 B.C. The Guanches lived by hunting, herding, farming, and fishing. In the late 1400s, the islands became a Spanish **colony**. Most Guanches not killed by the Spanish or by European diseases were enslaved, and this ancient people died out in the 1500s. The Canaries became the last port of call for Spanish ships setting out across the Atlantic, including those of Christopher Columbus. They remained important for shipping until the mid-1800s. Today, the mainstays of the island economy are farming and tourism.

The Spanish colonial city of Santa Cruz clusters above the harbor in Tenerife, one of the Canary Islands.

In the 1960s, grass-covered mounds at L'Anse aux Meadows in Newfoundland were found to be the remains of buildings in a one-thousand-year-old Viking settlement. The settlement, which has been reconstructed at its original site (above), *probably was used for only about ten years.*

Migration across the Atlantic

The open Atlantic formed an uncrossable barrier to most early coastal peoples. They fished inshore waters but generally lacked the navigation and boat-building skills needed to venture far beyond sight of land. The Vikings of Scandinavia were probably the first people to sail right across the ocean. Around A.D. 1000, these fierce seafarers crossed the North Atlantic and briefly settled the coasts of what are now Newfoundland, Labrador, and Maine.

By the 1400s, European nations on the shores of the Atlantic had developed the shipbuilding and navigation skills needed to make long ocean voyages. They began to venture along Atlantic coasts

and out into open waters in search of new lands, riches, and trading connections. In the late 1400s, Portuguese sailors rounded the southern tip of Africa to reach the Indian Ocean and the East Indies in Asia. Ships from Portugal were soon making regular voyages to the East to bring back silks and spices. Other nations, including Spain, Britain, and France, tried to find new sea routes to Asia by sailing west across the Atlantic.

European Colonization

In 1492, Italian explorer Christopher Columbus became the first European to reach the Americas since the Vikings. He landed in the Bahamas, which he mistook for the East Indies in Asia, and made contact with the Arawak people there. By the early 1500s, Europeans had charted the entire western coast of the Atlantic. Wherever they found natural harbors in these new lands, they set up trading posts. These posts soon grew into larger settlements, protected by forts.

As they spread inland, Europeans claimed as colonies the Americas—which they termed the "New World"—and Africa. They fought wars with local peoples and against each other to increase these territories. Huge quantities of gold, ivory, furs, and other riches on their way to Europe passed through the new Atlantic ports the colonists had founded.

Almost all lands that edged the Atlantic in Africa and the Americas became European colonies. Coastal lands

European colonists have left their mark on all Atlantic coasts. This castle on the coast of Ghana in Africa was a trading center for gold and slaves in the 1600s.

in Central and South America were claimed by Spain and Portugal. Britain established thirteen colonies along the east coast of North America. The first lasting settlement there was at Jamestown, Virginia, on the land of the Powhatan people. Canada was divided between France and Britain. Native Americans not killed in war were often enslaved. Millions died from diseases brought by Europeans, to which Native Americans had no natural resistance.

Transatlantic Trade

From the mid-1500s onward, ships bringing European colonists began to cross the Atlantic Ocean in increasing numbers. Ships were soon bringing a new cargo to the Americas: African slaves. Several trading routes across the Atlantic Ocean included slaves. Ships left Europe, for example, ferrying alcohol, guns, and other metal goods to ports in West Africa. There, these cargoes were exchanged for African slaves, who were then transported across the ocean to work in plantations in the Americas and the Caribbean. Huge numbers of people died during the voyages because of the terrible conditions on the slave ships. The ships often returned to Europe bringing cotton, sugar, rum, and tobacco, which were sold for huge profits. An estimated ten million Africans had been shipped across the Atlantic by the time slavery was finally abolished throughout North and South America in the late 1800s (Brazil had slaves until 1888).

Settlers of All Races

In 1783, the United States of America won independence from Britain. The Spanish and Portuguese empires in the Americas broke up in the early 1800s. Canada became self-governing in 1867. European nations held onto their claims in Africa for much longer, but throughout the course of the 1900s, African lands bordering the Atlantic Ocean became part of independent nations.

European influence, however, lives on into modern times in former colonies along Atlantic coasts—in the culture, religion, and often the language of the inhabitants. Many peoples of the western Atlantic are largely or partly descended from settlers of all races who arrived in colonial times.

Ports and Cities

Trade boomed across the North Atlantic in the 1800s. Sheltered inlets that made good harbors grew into busy ports and then into great cities, such as New York City, Boston, and New Orleans in the United States. Across the ocean, ports such as Bilbao in Spain, Lisbon in Portugal, Bordeaux in France, and Bristol in Britain also grew in size. Wide rivers—including the St. Lawrence and Mississippi in North America and the Amazon in South America—allowed ships to reach cities far inland. The Brazilian port of Manaus, for example, lies 1,240 miles (2,000 km) up the Amazon River.

Following the Industrial Revolution in the 1700s and 1800s, many of the world's chief industrial nations grew up on the shores of the North Atlantic. Ports such as New York City became great industrial centers as factories sprang up to process raw materials brought from

The European nation of Portugal was a leader in the exploration and colonization of the Atlantic. Lisbon, shown here in a sixteenth-century print, was one of many European ports on the Atlantic that flourished with the transatlantic shipping trade.

New York City

New York City, one of the United States' largest ports, lies at the mouth of the Hudson River. Four hundred years ago, this fine natural harbor was surrounded by rolling hills and farmland. In the 1800s, extensive deepwater docks were built around Manhattan Island. Flour mills, factories, and chemical plants grew up all around the port to process the raw materials that arrived by sea or river. As ships grew larger in the 1900s, the docks were moved to the nearby mainland so that **supertankers** and other large vessels could dock there. Manhattan, today bristling with skyscrapers, lies at the heart of a vast, sprawling city. More than eighteen million people now live in the New York metropolitan area.

A 1941 photograph shows the fish market on the water-front of Manhattan. New York City is still one of the world's twenty largest ports in terms of traffic and cargo.

abroad. Over the centuries, cargoes carried across the Atlantic also changed. Following the Industrial Revolution, raw materials and manufactured goods became the main Atlantic cargoes.

Development of Coastlines

The coastlines of the South Atlantic generally remained less developed than those bordering the North Atlantic, at least until the late 1800s and 1900s. Many settlements on southern coasts are still small fishing villages or vacation destinations. Some South American ports, however, such as Rio de Janeiro in Brazil and Buenos Aires in Argentina, have grown into sprawling cities.

In northwest and southwest Africa, long stretches of Atlantic coastline are too dry and barren to become heavily populated and industrialized. The fertile coasts of West Africa around the equator have many sizeable cities, however, including Accra in Ghana, Dakar in Senegal, and Lagos in Nigeria. Over 85 percent of Nigeria's industries are located in Lagos. At present, only a fraction of West Africa's population lives in coastal cities, but this is changing rapidly as more people move to the coast.

CHAPTER FIVE

TRANSPORTATION AND COMMUNICATION

Since the 1500s, the Atlantic has been the world's busiest ocean for trade and shipping. The first ships to navigate the open ocean were the wooden vessels of the Vikings, each powered by a single square sail and oars. By the late 1400s, European shipbuilders were constructing sailing ships called carracks and caravels for voyages of

exploration. During the 1700s and 1800s, the shipyards of North America and Europe competed to produce fast sailing ships, such as clippers, to ferry cargo across the ocean. By the mid-1800s, the first steamships were crossing the Atlantic, and these soon replaced sailing ships.

Modern Transportation

Modern vessels use various means of propulsion, including electric, natural gas, diesel, and nuclear-powered engines. A voyage across the Atlantic, once a long and difficult journey lasting many weeks, now takes just a few days.

The year 1919 saw the dawn of a new era of Atlantic travel, as the first aircraft crossed the ocean. Regular flights were soon operating between Europe and North America. The early 1900s were the age of giant ocean liners, but by the 1950s it had become cheaper and quicker to travel by airplane.

Huge container ships, such as this one at Port Elizabeth, New Jersey, carry boxcar sized cargo across the Atlantic.

Today's Cargoes

Today, a high proportion of modern **freight**, including farm produce that only stays fresh for a short time, travels by air. Bulky and heavy cargoes, such as minerals and machinery, still go by sea. Many goods are carried by **container** ships that are quick to load and unload at ports. Today, one-third of all ships crossing the Atlantic are oil tankers bringing fuel to industrialized nations.

Shortcuts to Other Oceans

Once, all ships traveling between the Atlantic and Indian Oceans had to go by way of South Africa and the Cape of Good Hope. The opening of the Suez Canal in Egypt in 1869 reduced the journey by thousands of miles. Similarly, ships sailing between the Atlantic and Pacific

Sinking

12:26 A.M.: "We have collision with iceberg. Sinking."

1:10 A.M.: "We are in collision with berg. Sinking head down. . . . Come soon as possible."

1:30 A.M.: "We are putting passengers off in small boats. . . . Women and children in boats, can not last much longer."

1:45 A.M.: "Come as quickly as possible old man: the engine-room is filling up to the boilers."

Radio messages from the Titanic *to other ships just before sinking on April 15, 1912*

The *Titanic*

Icebergs are a serious danger in the northwest Atlantic, in a zone known as "Iceberg Alley." The most famous disaster in this region was the loss of the *Titanic* in 1912. The luxury liner struck an iceberg on her first voyage from Britain to New York and sank in under three hours. About fifteen hundred passengers and crew perished.

The Titanic *leaves Belfast, Northern Ireland, for a test voyage in 1912.*

Oceans used to go by way of Cape Horn at the tip of South America. The Panama Canal, cut through the narrow neck of Panama in Central America, opened in 1914, providing a significant shortcut.

Dangerous Waters

Hazards to shipping in the Atlantic include strong currents, huge waves, submerged reefs and **shoals**, and storms and hurricanes. Icebergs in far northern Atlantic waters have wrecked many ships, including the *Titanic* in 1912. Treacherous currents and towering waves off Namibia in southwest Africa have led to many

shipwrecks on what is termed the
"Skeleton Coast." In the western
Atlantic, the shifting shoals and sandbars
of Sable Island, off Cape Sable, have
wrecked so many vessels that this area is
called the "Graveyard of the Atlantic."

Navigation and Communication Systems

The first sailors to navigate the Atlantic
used their knowledge of wind, waves,
and currents to find their way across
open seas. The positions of the Sun, the

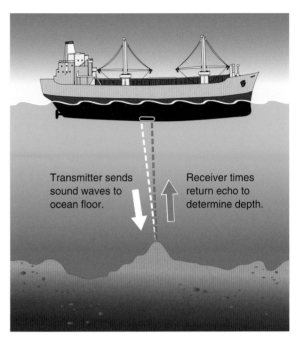

*Sonar works with a transmitter that aims pulses of sound
waves at the seabed. A receiver times how long the echoes
take to bounce back. The length of time indicates the depth.*

Moon, and stars helped sailors keep track
of their locations at sea.

About 1200, the invention of magnetic
compasses allowed sailors to find their
direction. In the 1500s, instruments such
as the cross staff and the sextant made it
easier to measure the position of the Sun
and stars. This ability allowed sailors to
calculate their latitude. Finding **longitude**
was made possible by the invention of the
chronometer in the 1770s.

Modern ships are equipped with
a wide range of instruments that show
them where they are and help to navigate
treacherous waters. These include **sonar**
and **radar**. Ship-to-shore radios allow
ships to maintain regular contact with
ports and weather stations. Modern

Transatlantic Cables

People have been communicating
across the Atlantic Ocean since the
first transatlantic cable was linked up
in 1858. Messages were sent along
the cable using telegraph, a system
that transmits electrical signals along
wires in codes tapped out on a telegraph machine. The first lasting
cable, completed in 1866, stretched
from Newfoundland to Ireland. The
first submarine cable for telephone
service across the Atlantic appeared
much later, in 1956. It ran from
Newfoundland to Scotland and was
used until 1978, by which time other
cables had been laid. That first cable
had thirty-six telephone lines. In
1988, the first fiber optic cable laid
in the Atlantic was able to carry forty
thousand telephone calls at a time.

compasses and global positioning systems (GPS) help ships pinpoint their positions using **satellites**. Satellites also help provide telephone communication across the huge distances of the ocean.

Undersea Travel

Pioneered in the 1800s, submarines developed rapidly during World War I. Other important submersibles were built and tested in Atlantic waters. In 1929, American naturalist Charles William Beebe (1877–1962) designed a new craft called a bathysphere, which was able to withstand the enormous pressure of the ocean depths. In 1930, Beebe and his partner Otis Barton descended to a depth of 200 feet (60 m) off the island of Bermuda. Four years later, the pair reached 3,000 feet (914 m). Beebe's record was broken by later dives in the Pacific, but his craft helped pioneer a new generation of submersibles, such as *Alvin*, built at the Woods Hole Oceanographic Institution in Massachusetts and launched in 1964.

Salvage and Treasure

From early times, the lure of sunken treasure ships acted as a spur to under-sea travel. In Atlantic waters, a historic **salvage** mission was led by Captain William Phips in 1687. Phips's team recovered treasure from a Spanish vessel that sank off Cuba forty years earlier. The divers used an air-filled, weighted barrel to which they returned for air.

Alvin, one of the most active and successful submersibles, has made over 3,600 dives since 1964. It can dive to over 14,500 feet (4,400 m).

In the 1980s, U.S. salvage experts searched for the wreck of the *Titanic* on the bed of the North Atlantic. In 1985, Robert Ballard found the vessel using a submarine sled called *Argo*, which was equipped with cameras. The following year, Ballard returned in the submersible *Alvin* and explored the *Titanic* using a robot named "Jason Junior." Today, undersea exploration and salvage work are also carried out by unmanned submersibles, ships with drilling equipment, sonar, and even satellites.

CHAPTER SIX

RESOURCES

Fish and shellfish are vital Atlantic Ocean resources. Other resources found in the Atlantic are minerals, such as oil and iron ore. The ocean itself, with its coastlines, islands, and waves, is a resource for vacationers, sailors, and swimmers.

A school of yellow fin tuna travels through the Atlantic along the Gulf Stream. Tuna are fished in large numbers by commercial fishing fleets.

Commercial Fishing

The Atlantic has always provided fish and shellfish for the people on its shores. The shallow waters of continental shelves and underwater ridges are the most productive areas. The Atlantic contains some of the world's richest fishing grounds, including the Grand Banks off the coast of Newfoundland, Georges Bank off Cape Cod, and Dogger Bank in the North Sea. Upwellings off the coasts of West Africa and southern Africa are also rich in marine life.

The first European explorers to sail the northwest Atlantic observed huge stocks of cod around the Grand Banks of Canada. From the 1500s onward, English, French, and Portuguese fishing boats crossed the ocean to harvest these rich fishing grounds. From those early times right through to the late 1900s, the North Atlantic was the world's most heavily fished ocean.

The main species of fish caught in the North Atlantic are cod, haddock, herring, plaice, and flounder. Hake, tuna, and herring are fished in the South Atlantic. Waters chilled by cold currents off Africa hold huge stocks of surface-dwelling sardines and anchovies. Shellfish, such as lobster, shrimp, and crab, are harvested off the shores of Maine, north Brazil, and West Africa.

Today, 90 percent of the total catch is harvested by commercial fishing fleets. Some of these are from bordering nations, others from faraway countries, such as Japan.

In the second half of the twentieth century, the number of commercial fleets operating in the Atlantic more than doubled. In the 1960s, a new generation of modern "factory" **trawlers** appeared. These boats had giant nets that could harvest vast numbers of fish at once. The fish were frozen and stored in large holds, which meant the ships could stay at sea for months on end, continuously catching fish.

Overfishing

By the 1980s, fish stocks in some parts of the Atlantic were in serious trouble. So many fish had been caught that not enough were left to breed. In 1992, experts discovered that the cod stocks of Newfoundland had shrunk to just 1 percent of what they had been in the 1960s. Canada closed its cod fishing industry, with the loss of forty thousand jobs. Around the same time, experts realized that stocks of Atlantic salmon off Greenland, in addition to several species in the North Sea, were failing because of overfishing. The nations of the North Atlantic decided that fish catches needed to be carefully controlled to prevent the ocean from being fished out.

Whaling

The history of whaling in the Atlantic reflects a similar story of overuse of ocean resources. Whale hunting began in the North Atlantic in the 1600s and boomed until the 1800s. The whalers operated from Europe and from stations along the northeastern United States. Whales were killed for their meat and their fatty blubber, which was used to make lamp oil, soap, and food. Baleen from the

Lobster boats sit in the harbor at Bar Harbor, a port on the Maine coast in the North Atlantic. About four thousand lobster boats operate in the Gulf of Maine.

Energy from the Atlantic

The Atlantic is rich in energy sources, such as **fossil fuels**. Oil and natural gas are mined in the North Sea, off the coast of West Africa, and in the Gulf of Mexico. Energy can also be harnessed from the power of the ocean itself. The rise and fall of the tide is used to generate electricity at tidal power stations in the Bay of Fundy and at the mouth of the Rance River in France, where a giant dam has been built across the river. As the tide ebbs and flows, the water spins **turbines** that generate electricity. Scientists are currently working on ways to harness wave energy. They are also trying to utilize temperature differences in ocean water of various depths, making energy by using a technique called ocean thermal energy conversion.

This oil rig is in the North Sea, an area of the Atlantic rich in oil deposits.

whales' mouths was used to make ladies' corsets, umbrellas, brushes, and other products.

In the late 1800s, the invention of **harpoon** guns made whales even easier to target. When large species—such as the right, humpback, and blue whales—became scarce, the whalers went after smaller species. When whale numbers dropped in the North Atlantic, the whalers moved to the South Atlantic. By the 1960s, there were very few large whales left in any part of the ocean.

In the 1980s, commercial whaling was banned worldwide in an effort to save many types of whales from extinction. Some whale species have since begun to recover, but others are still scarce. Only around eight thousand bowhead whales, for example, are thought to survive.

Mining the Ocean

Some parts of the Atlantic are rich in minerals, including titanium, a metallic element, and zircon, used to make gems. Tin and iron ore are mined off central Africa. Some of the world's best-quality diamonds are **dredged** from the coastal waters of Namibia, where rivers wash them out to sea. Most ocean mining is done in the shallow waters of continental shelves, because dredging and drilling are very difficult in deep water. Geologists, however, are

Tourists crowd a popular beach at Ponta Negra in Natal on Brazil's Atlantic coast.

currently investigating the possibility of mining parts of the deep ocean, for example the Mid-Atlantic Ridge.

Sand and gravel are dredged from shallow waters for use in construction, and some ten million tons of gravel are harvested from the North Sea every year. The Great Bahamas Bank yields a fine sand called aragonite, which is used to make glass and cement. Salt is extracted from seawater on some coasts. The seawater is channeled into shallow pans where the water evaporates, leaving salt crystals. About a century ago, geologists discovered manganese nodules—lumps of rock containing valuable minerals— lying on the bed of the deep oceans. No one, however, has yet come up with a practical way of collecting the nodules.

Tourism and Leisure

Atlantic coasts and islands are of major importance for the tourist industry. Resorts and vacation homes cover much of the east coast of the United States. In the South Atlantic, tourism is big business in areas including Rio de Janeiro in Brazil and Gambia in West Africa. Every year, millions of vacationers visit Atlantic islands, such as the Canaries and Bermuda, to enjoy activities such as boating, fishing, and swimming.

CHAPTER SEVEN

ENVIRONMENT AND THE FUTURE

For centuries, people have used the Atlantic Ocean for food and transportation. More recently, they have begun to mine the ocean's minerals. People also use the Atlantic to dump all kinds of waste. When coastal populations were smaller, this didn't matter so much, but now many millions of people live around the Atlantic. Pollution from the waste they throw away is harming the ocean **environment** and marine life.

Pollution along the Coasts

The coastal waters of the Atlantic are more affected by pollution than the deep,

open ocean. This is because much of the waste comes from seaside ports, cities, and factories as well as rivers that empty into the sea. The most polluted parts of the Atlantic include the North Sea, the northeastern shores of the United States, and the Santos estuary in Brazil.

Atlantic pollution has many causes. Cities produce large quantities of **sewage**. Factories on coasts and rivers release waste chemicals into the water. Chemicals used on farmers' fields drain off into rivers and end up in the sea. Mining and the burning of coal contribute to mercury levels in the environment. Mercury enters the food chain when it is absorbed by Atlantic fish and can reach levels dangerous to humans who consume the fish.

Dead Zones and Red Tides

Fertilizers cause floating **algae** to bloom, or multiply, rapidly. The excessive number

Air pollution hovers over the harbor at Boston, New England's biggest port. Industry and population growth along the Atlantic coast affect the ocean environment.

of algae reduce ocean oxygen levels, creating "dead zones" where sea grasses, fish, and other marine life die off.

Along the Atlantic coast of New England, the spread of harmful algae, or "red tides," reached peak levels in 2005. Nutrients runoff from farms on land and coastal fish farms can encourage these algal blooms, which are then carried by currents to other areas. Red-tide algae produce toxins that enter the food chain when eaten by clams, oysters, or mussels. The contaminated shellfish can then poison the fish and people who eat it.

Polluting the Open Oceans

The open oceans are also polluted by waste, dumped both accidentally and on purpose. In the late 1900s, the United States, Britain, and other industrialized

Spreading of the Red Tide

"Southern New England has just experienced a massive harmful algal bloom, or red tide, that was the worst in the region for at least thirty years. . . . The toxic cells that caused this bloom were more numerous and spread farther than ever before. We are concerned that the species may have colonized new areas and extended its range of impact."

Donald M. Anderson, lead investigator in the 2005 Atlantic red tide outbreak, Woods Hole Oceanographic Institution, July 2005

A foam of chemical pollutants washes from the North Sea onto a beach along the coast of the Netherlands in northern Europe.

nations dumped thousands of tons of dangerous **nuclear waste** into the Atlantic. Other industries also took garbage and harmful waste and dumped or burned it far out to sea.

Oil tankers cause pollution when they clean their tanks with seawater and flush oil into ocean waters. Major oil spills have occurred when tankers are damaged or wrecked in accidents. In November 2002, the oil tanker *Prestige* sank off the coast of northwest Spain. By 2003, about 64,000 tons of oil had leaked into the Atlantic from the *Prestige*, creating many oil slicks, killing thousands of birds, and poisoning marine life.

Fighting Pollution

In recent years, scientists and environmental groups, such as Greenpeace, have

Fish farms, such as this salmon farm in Scotland, help to reduce the threat to marine life in the Atlantic.

life has become seriously threatened by fishing and other human activities. Fish stocks in the ocean are disappearing rapidly because of overfishing. Governments have now imposed quotas, or limits, on the numbers of fish that can be caught.

Fish farming is also helping to ease the pressure on wild fish stocks. Salmon and sea trout are raised in pens and cages on the coasts of Canada, Scotland, and Scandinavia. Tuna are farmed in Nova Scotia. Oysters, mussels, and clams are raised on eastern shores of the United States and in France and Spain. Farmed fish and shellfish are now a significant part of the total Atlantic catch.

warned of the dangers of dumping waste at sea. Many North Atlantic nations have passed strict laws to reduce pollution. The rules are sometimes broken, however, and accidents still happen. In the South Atlantic, developing nations are gradually producing more pollution as their industries develop, but their governments often lack the funds to deal with waste and to develop cleaner industries.

Preserving Fish Stocks

In the last century or so, Atlantic marine

Preventing Extinction

Many people are active in conservation, hoping to save wildlife from harm or extinction, but much is at risk. Ridley and green turtles are now rare because so many have been killed for their meat, shells, and eggs. In addition, resorts on Atlantic beaches disturb the turtles' breeding habits.

Among marine mammals, seals and coastal otters have been hunted for their fur. In the 1800s and 1900s, millions of fur seals in the far north and south of the Atlantic were slaughtered for fur. Conservation groups managed to convince many people that this killing was wrong. Similar campaigns have helped save whales, such as the northern right whales, which were becoming extinct.

Atlantic marine life is protected when marine parks and reserves are set up. Many nations around the Atlantic have now passed laws to protect the rare plants and animals living off their shores.

The Future of the Atlantic Ocean

The future of the Atlantic's wildlife and the millions of people that inhabit its shores will depend on several factors. To keep the ocean healthy, the best ways to use its resources must be found. As fish farming increases, for example, it will reduce overfishing, but it will also introduce chemicals into the ocean that harm marine life. Wind turbines will be used increasingly along Atlantic coasts and just offshore to create electricity. The turbines will produce clean energy, but they will disrupt marine habitats.

Climate change will play a large part in the future of the Atlantic Ocean. Since 1995, Atlantic hurricanes have become increasingly fierce and frequent. Scientists believe this may be part of a cycle caused by changing water temperatures and ocean patterns, and they say the high storm activity could last until at least 2020. As global warming causes longterm temperature changes, the climate of the Atlantic Ocean may alter significantly, bringing changes that affect many parts of the world.

Global Warming

A climate change identified in recent years is affecting the world's oceans. World temperatures are slowly but steadily rising, in part because of air pollution from the burning of fossil fuels. Gases given off when these fuels burn trap the Sun's heat, producing warmer weather. The rising temperatures are warming the oceans, which makes the water expand and so raises sea levels. Land ice in polar regions is already melting into the oceans because of warmer temperatures, and this could dramatically raise sea levels. If the Atlantic Ocean rises by several feet, low-lying coasts —in Florida, for example—may be flooded, and islands could disappear. Scientists also believe that global warming will bring more storms and hurricanes. It could affect the circulation of water in the oceans, making the Gulf Stream, for example, change course. This change would have a significant effect on the climate of some North Atlantic regions. Many nations around the world, however, are making an effort to address global warming by reducing energy consumption and cutting down on air pollution.

TIME LINE

Before 100,000 B.C. People inhabit Atlantic coasts of Africa.

By 40,000 years ago People inhabit Atlantic coasts of Europe.

By 15,000 years ago People inhabit Atlantic coasts of North and South America.

100 B.C. Guanches settle Canary Islands.

A.D. 800s–1000 Viking explorers establish colonies on Iceland, Greenland, and eastern shores of North America.

About 1200 Invention of magnetic compass.

1488 Portuguese sailor Bartolomeu Dias explores the Atlantic coast of Africa and rounds the Cape of Good Hope.

1492 Italian explorer Christopher Columbus reaches the Bahamas, seeking India on a voyage for Spain.

Early 1500s European sailors and fur traders begin to cross North Atlantic for resources from eastern North America.

Late 1500s Transportation of African slaves to the Americas begins.

1600s British colonies are founded on east coast of North America.

1687 Captain William Phips leads salvage mission to recover treasure from sunken Spanish vessel in Atlantic.

1783 United States of America wins independence from Britain.

Early 1800s Spanish and Portuguese empires in the Americas break up.

1800s Shipping trade booms across Atlantic.

Mid-1800s Steamships begin crossing Atlantic.

1840s to early 1900s Large numbers of European settlers emigrate to United States.

1867 Canada becomes a self-governing part of British Empire.

1869 Suez Canal opens.

Late 1800s Invention of harpoon gun used for whale hunting leads to scarcity of whales. Slavery ends in Americas.

1912 Ocean liner *Titanic* sinks in the North Atlantic after hitting an iceberg.

1914 Panama Canal opens.

1919 First airplane crosses Atlantic Ocean.

1929 U.S. naturalist Charles William Beebe designs bathysphere.

1960s Modern factory trawlers begin working in Atlantic fishing grounds.

1964 Submersible *Alvin* is launched.

1977 First hydrothermal vents are discovered.

Late 1900s Large amounts of radioactive nuclear waste are dumped in Atlantic Ocean by industrialized nations.

1980s Commercial whale hunting is banned worldwide.

1980s–1990s Fish stocks in Atlantic Ocean are found to be seriously depleted.

1985 U.S. marine scientist Robert Ballard locates and explores wreck of the *Titanic*.

2002 Oil tanker *Prestige* sinks off coast of Spain, causing oil slicks and harming marine life.

2005 Hurricanes Katrina, Rita, and Wilma damage communities along the Gulf of Mexico.

GLOSSARY

abyssal zone ocean below 6,600 feet (2,000 m)

algae tiny, simple plants or plant-like organisms that grow in water or damp places

barrier island island lying parallel to the shore that protects mainland from the open ocean

bathyal zone mid-depths of ocean water between 330–660 feet deep and 6,600 feet deep (100–200 m deep and 2,000 m deep)

cape point of land that juts out into water

colony territory claimed by a nation or area occupied by settlers

condense change from gas into liquid

container large crate—used on ships, trains, and trucks—that combines many smaller pieces of freight into one shipment for efficient loading and unloading

continental drift theory that landmasses are not fixed but slowly drift across Earth's surface because of tectonic plate movement

crustacean class of animals that has an outer shell and segmented body and that includes shellfish

current regular flow of water in a certain direction

delta land composed of mud and sand deposited around the mouth of a river

dredge gather by scooping up or digging out

environment surrounding conditions in which living things exist

equator imaginary line around the middle of Earth lying an equal distance between the North Pole and South Pole

estuary area of water at a coastline where a river meets the ocean

euphotic zone upper layer of ocean water, usually defined as above 330–660 feet (100–200 m)

evaporation process of change from liquid into gas

fossil fuel coal, oil, natural gas, and other fuels formed in the ground from remains of plants or animals

freight cargo transported by sea, air, rail, or road

gulf large inlet of an ocean

gyre surface current in an ocean or sea that moves in a clockwise or counterclockwise circle

habitat type of place, such as a mountain or coral reef, where plants and animals live

harpoon type of spear used for hunting large fish and whales

hydrothermal vent hot spring found in volcanically active parts of the ocean floor

lagoon shallow area of water near a larger body of water

latitude distance north or south of the equator

lava hot, melted rock on Earth's surface that has welled up from under the ground

longitude distance east or west of the prime meridian

low pressure atmospheric system that produces unstable, stormy weather. (High pressure produces stable weather with clear skies.) Air pressure is the weight of the atmosphere pressing down on Earth at any given point.

magma molten rock beneath the surface of Earth

mantle part of Earth between the crust and core. It is mostly solid rock, but part of it is molten.

marsh wet, usually grassy land

migration movement from one place to another

mineral natural, non-living substance

mollusk group of animals with thin, sometimes soft shells, including clams, octopus, and snails

navigation use of animal instinct or scientific skills to determine a route or steer a course

nuclear waste leftover product of the nuclear energy industry

overfishing catching so many fish that stocks are depleted or species made extinct

photosynthesis process in which plants use carbon dioxide, hydrogen, and light to produce food

plankton microscopic plants (phytoplankton) and animals (zooplankton) that float at the surface of oceans and lakes and provide food for many larger animals

polyp small sea animal with tube-like body and tentacles that attaches to rock or other substance

prevailing wind main wind in a particular region

radar system that detects and locates objects by bouncing radio waves off them

reef chain of rock or coral or raised strip of sand in water

ridge raised area on land or on ocean bottom

rift opening on land or in the ocean where the ground has split apart

salvage saving or recovering objects, such as treasure from a shipwreck

satellite vehicle that orbits Earth that can be used to send signals to Earth for communica-tions systems; or any object in space that orbits another, larger object

sediment loose particles of rocky material, such as sand or mud

sewage dirty water from homes and factories containing chemicals and human waste

shingle deposit of small rocks, like large gravel, usually found on coastlines

shoal bank of sand just below the water surface in an ocean or sea

sonar (short for sound navigation and ranging) system that uses sound waves to measure ocean depth and detect and locate underwater objects

spit long, narrow finger of land stretching out into water

subduction zone region where two tectonic plates press together, causing one to subduct, or dive below the other

submersible small underwater craft often used to explore deep parts of the ocean

subpolar in or having to do with the region of the world just outside the polar regions

supertanker very large ship fitted with tanks for carrying liquid

temperate in or having to do with the regions of the world that lie between the Tropics and the polar regions

trawler vessel that drags a large net to catch fish

tropical in or having to do with the region of the world known as the Tropics

Tropics region of the world either side of the equator between the tropic of Cancer and the tropic of Capricorn

turbine engine, powered by steam, gas, or other force, that spins to generate electricity

upwelling periodic rise of dense, cold water to the ocean's surface when warmer surface waters are pulled away by currents

FURTHER RESOURCES

Books

Innes, Brian. *Down to a Sunless Sea: The Strange World of Hydrothermal Vents*. Sagebrush, 2000.

Major, Mireille. *Titanic: Ghosts of the Abyss*. Hyperion, 2003.

Matsen, Brad. *The Incredible Record-Setting Deep-Sea Dive of the Bathysphere*. Incredible Deep-Sea Adventures (series). Enslow Publishers, 2003.

Oleksy, Walter. *Mapping the Seas*. Watts Library—Geography (series). Franklin Watts, 2002.

Petersen, David and Christine Petersen. *The Atlantic Ocean*. True Books: Geography (series). Children's Press, 2000.

Skelton, Olivia. *The Atlantic Coast*. Ecosystems of North America (series). Benchmark Books, 1999.

Vogel, Carole Garbuny. *Savage Waters*. The Restless Sea (series). Franklin Watts, 2003.

Woodward, John. *Midnight Zone*. Exploring the Oceans (series). Heinemann, 2004.

Web Sites

The Atlantic Ocean
www.aquatic.uoguelph.ca/oceans/AtlanticOceanWeb/frameset1.htm

Defenders of Wildlife—Marine
www.defenders.org/wildlife/new/marine.html

FEMA for kids: Hurricanes
www.fema.gov/kids/hurr.htm

How NASA Studies Water
kids.earth.nasa.gov/water.htm

JASON—Lost City Hydrothermal Vents—Kids' Corner
lostcity.jason.org/kids_corner.aspx

WWF Habitats Home
www.panda.org/news_facts/education/middle_school/habitats/index.cfm

About the Author

Jen Green worked in publishing for fifteen years. She is now a full-time author and has written more than 150 books for children about natural history, geography, the environment, history, and other topics.

INDEX

ml

5/06